OUTDOOR LIVING™

HUNTING

JOE GASPAR AND JACK WEAVER

ROSEN
PUBLISHING

NEW YORK

To the volunteer hunter/trapper education instructors throughout North America, who dedicate their time and energy to educate youth in the fundamentals of hunting and trapping —JW

Published in 2016 by The Rosen Publishing Group, Inc.
29 East 21st Street, New York, NY 10010

Copyright © 2016 by The Rosen Publishing Group, Inc.

First Edition

All rights reserved. No part of this book may be reproduced in any form without permission in writing from the publisher, except by a reviewer.

Library of Congress Cataloging-in-Publication Data

Gaspar, Joe.
  Hunting / Joe Gaspar and Jack Weaver.
    pages cm. — (Outdoor living)
  Includes index.
  Audience: Grades 7 - 12.
  ISBN 978-1-4994-6237-1 (library bound)
  1. Hunting—Juvenile literature. I. Weaver, Jack. II. Title.
  SK35.5.G37 2015
  639'.1—dc23
                    2015017873

Manufactured in China

CONTENTS

INTRODUCTION

More than thirteen million Americans go hunting every year. Hunting has been a popular outdoor acivity in North America for a long time.

*H*unters get to experience the great outdoors in a way that most other people do not. While others may observe animals and the ecosystems in which they live, hunters insert themselves into the food chain. Doing so reminds them of the closer ties that people had to the natural world in the past. It reminds them that human beings are part of nature, too.

Being a good hunter takes considerable skill and requires a lot of knowledge. Experienced hunters can recognize the tracks and scat of many species. They can recognize the signs—from broken branches to claw marks—that an animal has passed though. Hunters need to be smart and responsible. They must handle firearms carefully and should always follow hunting laws and regulations.

Hunting is a lot of fun—as well as a great way to spend time outside with people you care about. It is frequently a family activity; many people appreciate the way it brings different generations together. Experienced hunters enjoy sharing their skills with young people, who in turn value becoming part of a long tradition. Even if you do not have a family tradition of hunting, you can still enjoy being a hunter.

THE HISTORY OF HUNTING

Human beings first started hunting in order to get food. Hunting was a matter of survival. These days, though, most people—especially those in developed countries like the United States and Canada—buy their food from a store. While the vast majority of North Americans no longer need to hunt, that does not mean that hunting has died out. It has just gone from something that people do to survive to an activity they do in their free time for their own enjoyment. Hunters love the challenge that pursuing animals in the wilds of nature presents. They like how hunting connects them with nature and with the lifestyles of people in the past.

HUNTING FOR FOOD

The early American colonies were made up mostly of farmers. They

This mid-nineteenth-century lithograph by the American printmaking firm Currier and Ives shows two men returning home from a hunt with food for dinner.

ate some of the grains they grew and the livestock they raised. They also sold what they raised for money and goods. Little industry existed to provide the kinds of food markets that we have today. Because wild game was needed for food, the colonists decided that this bounty should belong to everyone and not just the landowners, as had been the case in Europe.

Unfortunately, wildlife and other natural resources were mistakenly thought to be inexhaustible. As pioneers pushed farther into the interior, an explosion of industry followed. Railroads and modern firearms were soon to wreak havoc on America's wildlife resources. Rather than merely providing meat for

NATIVE AMERICAN HUNTERS

Native Americans historically depended on hunting as an important source of food. In fact, hunting provided more than just food. The fur, bones, and other parts of the animal's body were also used in making clothing, shelter, tools, and household goods.

The kind of quarry that Native Americans caught depended on where they lived, but most animals were considered edible. Native Americans used several hunting techniques. Most hunting was done with a bow and arrows, but spears and traps were also used. Knives, which were generally made of bone or stone, were used to skin the animal and to cut up the meat.

frontier kitchens, hunting wildlife suddenly became a highly competitive industry. Armed with mass-produced firearms, market hunters shipped boxcar-loads of wild game to markets in the eastern United States.

Even before the turn of the twentieth century, America's wildlife resources were quickly becoming depleted. In the West, the buffalo and beaver were all but gone. In the East, elk, furbearers, large predators, waterfowl, and flocks of passenger pigeons—once so numerous that their migrations had darkened the sky—were also gone. Whitetail deer were so scarce that when a deer track was found, whole communities would get in their buggies and drive out to see it. Turkeys, grouse, and black bears were making their last stand in a few remote mountain ranges. Even the rugged hills of the Allegheny Mountains, once covered with virgin stands of giant oak, chestnut, white pine, and hemlock, were reduced to eroded, fire-swept ridges by the logger's axe.

THE RISE OF SPORT HUNTING

By the end of the nineteenth century, a new breed of hunter was emerging on the American scene. They called themselves sportsmen. In the early days of sport hunting, sportsmen were mostly rich and powerful people. They lamented the loss of the wild game they loved to hunt. They began to work for change and formed sportsmen's protective associations. As a result of their lobbying, individual states began to form wildlife agencies. Laws establishing seasons and bag limits on wildlife were enacted, and game wardens were hired to enforce those laws on behalf of all the citizens. These laws were not popular, and some game wardens were killed by hunters while trying to enforce these laws.

In the late 1930s, most state game agencies began to hire wildlife biologists, and a new era of scientific wildlife management was born. Modern wildlife management has been and still is a hard-fought battle against those who would destroy wildlife habitats through pollution and expanded development. Sport hunters have led the fight for wildlife conservation. This may seem like a contradiction, for sport hunters do indeed hunt and kill wildlife. However, they were the first to support laws that would protect

U.S. president Theodore Roosevelt, shown here hunting in Colorado, was an enthusiastic hunter and an important early supporter of the conservation movement.

wildlife against extinction. The sport hunters of America help pay the bill for wildlife management through hunting license fees, special excise taxes on hunting and fishing equipment, and donations of their time, money, and energy to help wildlife agencies and conservation groups develop wildlife habitats.

Thanks in part to sport hunters, North America is once again teeming with wildlife. Most wild game species are again plentiful, and in some cases abundant. Some species, like the buffalo and bald eagle, have been rescued from the brink of extinction and are now protected from being hunted. Very few animals on the endangered species list are game animals. Nor are these animals endangered because of sport hunting. Habitat losses due to urbanization and pollution are the key factors in the decline of wildlife species today.

Actually, sport hunting in North America has never been better. Although carefully managed by state game departments, big game of all types is abundant. Upland game birds are plentiful. Waterfowl hunting is very carefully monitored and managed by both the U.S. Fish and Wildlife Service and state wildlife agencies, and today most species of waterfowl are plentiful. With the exception of the eastern farming communities, small game hunting across the United States is relatively good, especially the hunting of woodland species.

THE WORLD OF SPORT HUNTING

Some of today's sport hunters are willing to travel long distances to pursue their sport. Eastern hunters travel west in pursuit of Rocky Mountain elk, bighorn sheep, mountain goats, antelope, mule deer, and mountain lions. Hunters gunning for ring-necked pheasants chase their prey in the Great Plains. Waterfowl hunters pursue ducks and geese in the pothole country of the Midwest or along the major flyways. Brown bears, caribou, and Dall sheep are found in Alaska. Northern whitetails, caribou, and moose are hunted in the Canadian provinces, while wild hogs are sought in Texas.

These hunters are pursuing moose in Alaska. Alaska is a world-class hunting destination, with a wide range of game species and habitats.

Nowadays more hunters than ever before are packing their bags and traveling to exotic places. Hunting trips are routinely booked to nearly all parts of the world, including South America, Asia, Australia, Russia, Africa, and the Arctic, in pursuit of everything from big cats to musk ox. One doesn't just hop on a plane and fly off to exotic places. Passports and visas are needed. So are lots of immunization shots. Ouch! In addition, a reputable outfitter who is familiar with such things as endangered species, hunting licenses, and importation laws is a must. Good outfitters will not only make your trip run smoother and know how to find the game, but they can also keep you out of foreign jails.

STARTING OUT

Beginning hunters should try learning the sport closer to home. For example, try hunting for rabbits or squirrels on a nearby woodlot, farm, or ranch. Many farmers allow hunters to use their woodland properties to hunt small game for a modest fee. As a beginner this will allow you to become familiar with simple firearms such as the common .22 caliber rifle. Dove or upland game bird hunting is also a sport for beginners who need to gain some experience before taking a trip into the big woods in pursuit of more challenging game. Before you can get started, however, you will need to know what kinds of equipment are available and which is the best to use for the game you will hunt.

WHAT YOU'LL NEED

Before you set off on a hunting trip, make sure that you have everything you'll need. First off, you'll need something to hunt with. This will generally mean a firearm. Shotguns and rifles are the types of firearms that hunters regularly use. You'll also need ammunition; a gun's no use if you don't have anything to shoot out of it! In most cases you'll also need a hunting license.

Since hunting takes place in the great outdoors, you'll need to be properly dressed and prepared for whatever weather you're likely to encounter. If you are hunting in an unfamiliar area, remember to bring along a map. You don't want to get lost in the woods!

RIFLES AND SHOTGUNS

One of the first things you'll need to decide is what kind of firearm to use. This depends entirely upon the game you intend to hunt.

Large-caliber rifles are used to hunt large game, such as bears, moose, and elk. Small-caliber rifles are used to hunt smaller animals, such as squirrels, raccoons, or prairie dogs. People use shotguns primarily to hunt waterfowl, game birds, and other small game.

Shotguns are the best option for people who want to hunt ducks and other waterfowl. There are even some shotguns designed specifically for waterfowl hunters.

The main difference between rifles and shotguns is the inside of their barrels. A rifle barrel has grooves cut inside. These grooves twist around the length of the rifle's barrel. Their purpose is to cause the bullet to spin or spiral much like the spin a quarterback puts on a football when he throws it. This allows the bullet to travel farther and be more accurate. A shotgun's barrel, on the other hand, is perfectly smooth inside.

Unlike a rifle, which fires one bullet at a time, a shotgun generally shoots a charge of small, round pellets called shot. This is why shotgun size is measured by gauge, which relates to the size of the

PICKING A SHOTGUN

Even once you've decided on a shotgun, many questions remain. Should you choose a mule-kicking 10-gauge, a 12-gauge, 16-gauge, 20-gauge, 28-gauge, or the snappy little .410 bore (sometimes mistakenly referred to as a .410 gauge)? Do you want a semiautomatic, pump action, bolt action, hinged action, double barrel, or single barrel? After deciding what type of shotgun you want, you may choose from several brands, depending on your budget. Of course, you should choose a properly choked barrel or barrels for your shotgun. Then come the decisions about ammunition. What size shot? What type of shot? What brand of shot? Or maybe you want rifled slugs instead?

shot charge that a particular shotgun is capable of handling. A rifle is measured by caliber, which is a measurement of the diameter of the bullet it can fire. Generally, however, the smaller the gauge, the bigger the diameter of the shotgun's barrel and the larger the shot charge it can fire. For rifles the opposite is true. The smaller the caliber, the smaller the bullet a particular rifle will fire. A .22 caliber rifle or a 20-gauge shotgun are good for beginners because they are easier to handle and have less recoil (or kickback).

THE RIGHT AMMUNITION

The type of ammunition you need depends on the firearm you are using and the quarry you intend to hunt. For example, be sure to match the caliber of rifle ammunition with the caliber of the firearm. Rifle ammunition is manufactured with different power loads and bullet tips designed for specific game species. Check with a reputable sporting goods dealer who deals with firearms and ammunition to purchase the correct match.

Shotgun ammunition is called shells. A shell is made up of a case that contains shot, gunpowder, a wad separating the shot from the gunpowder, and a primer that is struck to fire the shell. The shot is sometimes a single slug. More often, though, it consists of many small pellets. The size of the shot depends on the size of your quarry. Slugs are used in deer hunting. Shot sizes nine to seven and a half are generally used for quail, doves, or grouse. The carton the ammunition comes in will usually explain what game the shot size is effective for. Depending on the game you are hunting, you might choose lead, tin, bismuth, or steel shot pellets.

This hunter is loading one shell into each of the barrels of a double-barreled break-action shotgun. Break-action shotguns are also known as hinge-action shotguns.

Ammunition must be handled carefully and with respect for what it can do. A little .22 bullet can travel up to a mile and a half (2.5 kilometers). High-powered rifle ammunition can travel much farther. Although most shotgun ammunition is designed for shorter distances—generally under 50 yards (45 meters)—the pellets can travel much farther. In addition, bullets do not always stop when they hit something. Often they will pierce through their target and continue on.

WHAT TO WEAR

There is a lot of outdoor clothing available for today's hunters. Before you purchase clothing, check the hunting regulations for the area in which you intend to hunt. Some states have laws that regulate what hunters can wear. Whether you are looking for the latest in camouflage design or the brightest safety clothing, remember that you are going outdoors. Dress for the weather. In cold weather, layers of clothing are best. The outer garment should be water resistant or waterproof. On warm days, clothing that breathes will allow air to flow around you and prevent overheating. This type of clothing will also dry more quickly should you encounter a surprise shower or fall into a swamp. Generally speaking, jeans are not the best clothing to wear in the outdoors, especially when hunting.

Good boots are a must. Purchase the best ones you can afford. Waterproof is best, especially in colder weather. Hunting boots should extend over the ankles for good support in unstable terrain. They should have rugged soles for traction and wear. You will probably be out in all kinds of weather, and your boots should be comfortable yet rugged enough to handle it. Your feet are your transportation. If you treat them well, they will treat you well. There is nothing worse than wet, cold, and sore feet.

GETTING A GOOD LOOK

You need to be able to get a good view of your quarry to shoot it. This isn't usually a problem for hunters with shotguns. Shotguns don't have a very long range, so hunters need to get pretty close

Rifle scopes are available at different levels of magnification. A fixed power scope always magnifies by the same amount. The magnification on a variable power scope is adjustable.

to the animals they are pursuing. Rifles, on the other hand, have a much longer range. For this reason, many hunters mount scopes on their rifles. Hunters look through a scope—which looks a bit like a small telescope or one side of a pair of binoculars—to get a good view of their quarry.

Scopes make it easier to aim when you are shooting. When you look through a scope, you can see a pair of crossed lines—called the crosshairs or the reticle. The lines should cross on the very point you want the bullet to hit.

YOUR SURVIVAL KIT

Hunters should carry some sort of survival kit while hunting. Sporting goods stores stock survival kits that hold the basic needs should an emergency occur. A good survival kit should contain some basic first-aid items, a whistle, material for making a shelter, a small flashlight, extra food, and fire-starting materials, including waterproof matches.

Remember to bring along a map. Hunters often need to walk through unfamiliar forests, plains, and mountains. A good topographical map of the area a hunter plans to cover can help prevent him or her from getting lost. These maps give detailed information about everything from roads, trails, streams, and buildings to terrain elevation and the types of vegetation you may encounter. Also bring along compass or Global Positioning System (GPS)—a handheld computer that works with a navigational satellite to pinpoint the user's location on earth. Local topographical maps, compasses, and even GPSs can usually be purchased at sporting goods stores.

A sharp knife is also a necessity. In the case of knives, bigger is not always better. A knife with a blade no longer than 4 inches (10 centimeters) is fine. Buy a brand-name knife that is known for holding a keen edge. A dull knife is useless. When considering knives, look for a folding knife with a locking blade. A folding knife is safer and easier to carry, and the blade should lock in place when extended to prevent it from snapping shut on your fingers.

HUNTING LICENSES AND HUNTING LAWS

Every American state and Canadian province requires that hunters buy and carry a hunting license. Requirements for purchasing a hunting license vary and may be different for residents and nonresidents. Other considerations include age requirements for junior licenses and laws that state junior hunters must be accompanied by adults. You may also have to purchase a variety of required licenses, such as big or small game tags or specific species stamps. Check with your state's wildlife agency for licensing details.

You'll need to do some research to learn about your local hunting laws. One important thing to look into is what the hunting seasons are. These are the times of year you are allowed to hunt a particular animal. For example, most states have both spring and fall turkey-hunting seasons. Many states have separate seasons for hunting the same animal with different weapons, too. Find out if there is a separate hunting season for juvenile hunters. Youth seasons give you the opportunity to practice your hunting skills without having to compete with more experienced hunters.

During the spring turkey season, hunters can take only male turkeys, called toms or jakes. During the fall season, they are allowed to hunt either male or female turkeys.

TIPS FOR NEW HUNTERS

It's easy to be overwhelmed by the sheer amount of stuff you need to go hunting. Don't let this keep you from taking up the sport, though. For starters, you may be able to borrow a gun from a family member or a friend. If you do so, though, be sure to ask someone who is knowledgeable about firearms to check that the gun is safe and functions properly. You don't want to use an unsafe gun! Ammunition isn't that expensive, and most of the clothes used for hunting may also be worn for other outdoor pursuits, such as hiking, camping, or fishing.

DUCK STAMPS

While most U. S. hunting regulations are on the state level, there are federal laws that apply to waterfowl hunting. This is because most waterfowl migrate and are therefore protected by the Migratory Bird Treaty Act—which dates back to the 1910s and places limits on the hunting of migratory birds in the United States and Canada.

Each year, waterfowl hunters over the age of sixteen are required to purchase a duck stamp. Duck stamps grant their owners free admission to all national wildlife refuges. This is a big plus, since they are great places to go waterfowl hunting. The money from duck stamp sales helps fund the purchase of wetlands, providing important habitat for waterfowl and other animals.

Spend time outdoors, even outside of the hunting season. Go hiking. Walk around the area where you intend to hunt and become familiar with the lay of the land. Learn what animals live there and where they get their food. This is called scouting. If most of the wild land near you is posted against trespassing, you will need to get permission from the landowner first.

HUNTING TECHNIQUES

Just as there are many kinds of firearms and ammunition to choose from, there are also many different hunting techniques. Some techniques work better with certain kinds of game. Others are best suited to a particular habitat—such as flat grasslands or wooded foothills. Some require several people, while other work best for a solitary hunter. A hunter's personality will play a role in which method he or she prefers, too. That said, you won't know what you like best until you try several techniques.

STALKING YOUR QUARRY

Stalking may be the most common method of hunting. Stalking is done as it sounds: a hunter walks slowly and quietly through the woods looking for game. The key here is to know where your quarry is likely to be at any given time. You wouldn't want to be stalking through the high country if all the elk are in the lowlands. This is where preseason scouting and knowing your quarry come in handy. If you are after deer, for example, you will need to learn their feeding habits, where their feeding areas are, and when they move into or away from their feeding areas. You must also know where they are likely to shelter during stormy weather and where their bedding or resting areas are. For the restless hunter, stalking is a good technique.

GAME CALLS

Some hunters use calls to draw their quarry to them. In the case of turkeys, this means trying to imitate a hen in the spring or a lost member of the flock during the fall. Ducks and geese are generally called within the close range necessary for shotguns by trying to imitate the feeding sounds of other waterfowl. Still other game may be called in close by imitating the fighting sounds that male rivals make during breeding season. Bucks, for example, may be called by rattling antlers and using a grunt call. Bull elk and moose sometimes respond to the challenging bugles of their kind with explosive action. Predators such as coyotes, cougars, and foxes may be called by imitating their prey's distress calls or the distress calls of their young. The list doesn't end here.

Although anyone can learn to call game, doing so successfully takes considerable practice and patience. However, it is one of the most exciting and satisfying methods of hunting there is.

The adult hunter here is using a duck call. Duck calls can be used to make a variety of duck sounds, such as a basic quack, a comeback call, or a greeting call.

HUNTING STANDS

Hunting stands give you a vantage point from which to look down on your quarry, Stand hunting is popular, but it can be less exciting for a beginner. Hunting from a stand—whether it is a portable tree stand or some type of permanent stand—depends upon the stand itself being placed in the right location. Animal movement patterns vary over time because the woods are in a constant state of change. Just because someone has bagged a deer on a particular stand for the past ten years doesn't mean that spot will continue to produce.

There are several kinds of portable tree stands, including ladder stands, hang-on stands, and self-climbing stands. Each has its own advantages and disadvantages.

Again, scouting the area you intend to hunt is a must. Look for game trails, animal tracks, buck rubs or scrapes, droppings, and the availability of food.

HUNTING DECOYS

Some hunters lure animals to an area, and into a false sense of safety, by using decoys. Decoys are objects that are made to look like the animals being hunted. Deer and turkey decoys are fairly common, but the best-known decoys are probably the ones that look like waterfowl. Duck decoys, in particular, are known for being hard to distinguish from real ducks. If you're using decoys, it's important to set them up in a realistic manner. The arrangement of a group of

BLINDS

While stands make hunters harder for animals to notice by putting them up above eye level, blinds conceal hunters in a camouflaged shelter. There are many kinds of hunting blinds. Permanent blinds are usually built of wood and painted in hard-to-notice colors and patterns. Hunters build temporary blinds from grasses, sticks, branches, or any other material that will blend in with the surroundings. Portable blinds made out of net or fabric let you hide yourself in a different spot on every hunting expedition.

decoys is called a spread. You want your spread to look like a group of real birds. Take the direction of the wind and the current—if you are using floating decoys—into account when placing each decoy.

HUNTING WITH DOGS

Some hunters get a helping hand—or a helping paw—from dogs. Hunting dogs can be divided into two main groups: scent hounds and gun dogs. Scent hounds are dogs whose excellent sense of smell makes them skilled at tracking down hard-to-follow game by its scent alone. These dogs tend to have loud howls that help hunters follow them. They generally have a lot of endurance and can follow

This hunter and his dog are upland game hunting. Dogs are often used in upland game hunting. They are common in waterfowl hunting and raccoon hunting, too.

their quarry for long distances. Some kinds of hounds will corner an animal up a tree and wait for the hunter to arrive.

Gun dogs can be further divided into pointers, flushers, and retrievers. A pointer is trained to locate hard-to-find game—usually game birds like pheasant and quail—and alert a hunter to where it is by standing very still with its muzzle pointed toward the hidden quarry. Flushing dogs drive game out of its hiding place so that hunters can shoot it. Retrievers fetch game after it has been shot. They are often used in waterfowl hunting and are generally trained to carry the quarry back gently in their mouths so that the carcass does not get damaged. Gun dogs were bred to be easy to train and to get along well with people. These characteristics have made several breeds of gun dogs—including golden retrievers, Labrador retrievers, and cocker spaniels—popular as pets.

GAME DRIVES

For certain types of hunting, driving game is by far the most productive method. Driving game generally involves several hunters working together, although small drives can be done by as few as two hunters. When driving, a hunting party is divided into two groups, drivers and watchers. It is the drivers' job to get the game moving by traveling through the woods in a sort of skirmish line. The watchers are positioned at strategic points where the game is expected to go. Obviously, this takes a good deal of cooperation on the part of everyone involved and requires some serious safety considerations. It is an effective technique, especially for hunting whitetail deer.

BOW HUNTING

While shotguns and rifles are the most common hunting weapons, they aren't the only ones. Some hunters enjoy the challenge of bow hunting, or hunting with a bow and arrows. The bow and arrow is an ingenious invention. Basically, a flexible rod is rigged with a taught string that, when pulled back, creates a great force. This force shoots arrows much faster and farther than the human arm can throw a spear, knife, or rock.

COMPOUND BOWS

Bow hunting today uses the latest in materials and engineering technology. Bows are made of fiberglass or graphite materials. The vast majority of modern hunting bows are compound bows. Compound bows have wheels fitted on the ends of the bow. These wheels act as a pulley system to create greater tension when the string is pulled back. Compound bows supply hunters with faster arrow speed and a longer flying distance. Both give hunters a better chance against swift animals such as deer and rabbit.

The best feature of the compound bow, however, has to do with the draw weight, or how much force an archer needs to apply to pull the string all the way back. When an archer draws a compound bow's bowstring, he or she needs to apply the greatest amount of force at the halfway point. After the halfway point, amount of force required decreases dramatically to full draw. This enables archers to hold their aim longer, increasing aiming accuracy and the chance for a more precise shot.

The pulleys on either end of a compound bow are known as cams. Cables connect the cams to each other. The hunter holds the bow by the grip.

BOW HUNTING QUARRY

Bow hunters can hunt both small and large game. Blunt-headed arrows are used to hunt rabbit, grouse, hare, and squirrel. Bow fishing is also a popular sport. Barbed arrows tied to a string enable hunters to hook and reel in game fish such as trout, bass, and even shark! Bow hunters can also bring down big game, including elk, hogs, moose, deer, and turkey. Regulations exist in each state on when and how game can be hunted. You should always check state regulations before you begin each hunting season.

Bow hunters hunt either by stalking game or stand hunting. Bow hunting equalizes the challenge between hunters and prey. Bow hunters must be swift, steady, and silent. If you are looking for a challenge when you hunt, then bow hunting might be the hunting technique for you.

BE SMART, BE SAFE

When you are hunting, safety should always be your top priority. Irresponsible actions with a firearm—or with a bow for that matter—can kill or cause serious injury to people. Responsible hunters have a thorough understanding of how their firearms or bows work. They know all about the safety regulations in the areas they hunt in, as well as the common-sense safety precautions that all hunters should take around firearms.

TAKE A CLASS

One of the best ways to learn about hunting safety is to take a class on it. In fact, almost every state requires first-time hunters to complete a hunter education course sponsored by the state's wildlife agency. An identification card is issued to each successful graduate. This card must then be presented when purchasing a hunting license.

Qualified volunteers, under the supervision of state wildlife agencies, teach the courses. Courses generally require a minimum of ten hours or more to complete. Hunter education courses tend to include firearm handling and safety, ammunition identification and use, firearm safety in the home, bow hunting safety, hunter responsibility, game identification, survival, first aid, ethics, land-owner relations, game laws, and much, much more.

Most courses teach marksmanship and shooting fundamentals by offering live firing on ranges under the supervision of quali-fied range masters. Many also offer mock hunts that walk students through actual field courses.

Some schools teach hunting safety. This teen is learning about gun safety as part of the Hunter Education and Firearms Safety class at his school in Juneau, Alaska.

LEARNING ONLINE

Several states allow you to take part of your hunter safety course online. The purpose of home study is to give busy students the opportunity to complete the academic portion of the course in whatever free time they have. After successfully completing the written portion of the course, students then must complete their field days—the practical, hands-on portion of the course—under the supervision of course instructors.

To find out how to register for a hunter education course, contact your state wildlife agency or a local sportsman's club, or inquire at gun shops and sporting goods stores in your area.

START WITH THE BASICS

Hunting safety, like any safety issue, involves applying common sense when in the field. Hunter education addresses safety issues that concern the beginner and experienced hunter alike. Three basic rules of firearm safety sum it up best. Plant them firmly in your mind and follow them as if they were written in stone.

1. Treat every firearm as if it were loaded! Every firearm must be treated with respect. Assume every gun is loaded until you personally look into the action (those parts that load and fire a gun) to be sure it is not.

2. Always keep the muzzle pointed in a safe direction! The muzzle is the end of a firearm that the ammunition comes out of. Always keep the muzzle of your firearm pointed away from others. That way, should the gun be set off accidentally, no one will get hurt.

3. Be sure of your target! Legal game is the only target any hunter should be shooting at. Double-check your target before you pull the trigger.

EYE-CATCHING ORANGE

One way to stay safe when hunting is to wear clothing in the bright shade of orange that is known as blaze orange or hunter orange. Wearing blaze orange makes it easier for other hunters to spot you, but harder for them to mistake you for the quarry that they are pursuing. While the color is quite eye-catching to human beings, it doesn't stand out to some of the species that hunters commonly pursue, such as deer and elk.

You can buy blaze orange hats, shirts, vests, and more. States that say hunters must wear blaze orange often require them to wear a certain number of square inches of it.

Many states have laws that require hunters to wear blaze orange for certain kinds of hunting—especially big game hunting and upland game bird hunting. On the other hand, waterfowl hunters and turkey hunters are not generally required to wear blaze orange. Some choose to do so anyway, especially if they are hunting in an area where people are also hunting deer or upland game. After all, it's better to be safe than sorry!

STAYING SAFE IN A TREE STAND

Tree stands are a major source of hunting injuries. They are up in the air and can get slippery in wet or icy weather. It's easy to lose you balance, in particular when firing a gun. When the shotgun or rifle kicks, it can easily make a hunter move. Then—pow!—a slip and fall down through the rough limbs to the ground.

Portable tree stands involve particular dangers of their own. If they are not properly installed, they—and the people sitting on them—can come crashing down to the ground. Climbing up to or down from a tree stand can be treacherous, too. Hunters should never use portable tree stands without attaching themselves securely to the tree with a safety harness.

A LOT TO LEARN

Simply deciding that you want to go hunting is the first step in doing so. Taking a hunter education course is the second. Having done that, you will need a firearm or bow and arrows. Then you'll have to decide what quarry to pursue. Of course, it's also possible to decide what you want to hunt first and choose your firearm or bow with that in mind. These decisions are a lot easier to make if you know a bit about the firearm restrictions in your state or province—and if you have an experienced hunter to walk you through them. A mentor can help you become a better hunter, teaching you about everything from firearm safety to outdoor survival skills.

OBTAINING A FIREARM OR BOW

Because guns can be dangerous, there are age-based limits on who can own them. Federal law prohibits persons under eighteen from purchasing a shotgun or rifle. While people under eighteen cannot purchase these guns, they are permitted to own them. If, for example, your parents give you a shotgun as a sixteenth birthday present, that is not against the law. However, you should also check the law in your state. Some states impose further age-based restrictions on purchasing or owning guns.

If your parents decide to buy a gun for you, it's not a bad idea to go along and have some input. Since firearms are expensive, your family might want to consider a used shotgun or rifle. Most gun shops sell both new and used firearms. When purchasing a used firearm, make sure you buy it from a reputable gun shop that checks used firearms thoroughly before offering them for resale. If you are going to borrow a gun from a relative, neighbor, or friend, have it checked by someone familiar with that type of firearm to be sure it is safe before shooting it. More than one gun has exploded in the shooter's hands because someone accidentally left a cleaning patch inside the barrel. Especially check the safety mechanism (the part that blocks the trigger from firing prematurely) to be sure that it is working properly.

In most areas, there are not age restrictions on purchasing a bow. It's important to make sure the bow you select is the right size for you. You'll need to consider the bow's draw weight—how much force it takes to draw it—and its draw length—how far you need to pull the string back to draw the bow. Ask an experienced hunter to help you figure out what your draw length should be; figuring it out is not as easy as you might think.

FINDING A MENTOR

Traditionally, hunting was handed down from father to son as a part of a family's traditions. Today that has changed. On the plus side, more women are becoming involved in hunting and other

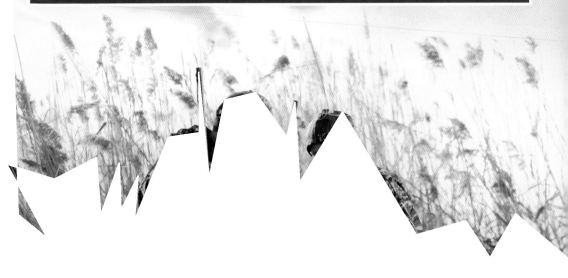

If your parents or grandparents are hunters, going hunting is a great way to spend time with them. This young hunter is learning about duck hunting from his father.

forms of outdoor recreation. However, hunting is not being pursued as actively as it once was. In some ways this is good for those who do hunt because more hunting opportunities are opening up. These are great times to be hunting! But it may be a little difficult for a beginner to find a mentor, especially since many parents no longer hunt.

Having a mentor is important. If your mom or dad is not a hunter, let your friends and relatives who do hunt know that you are interested in learning about hunting. They may offer to take you under their wing. After all, they know the ropes and maybe even belong to a hunting camp somewhere. If your relatives don't hunt, ask friends of the family. Don't just grab anybody, though. Make sure that your prospective mentor is trustworthy and responsible.

DOING THE RESEARCH

While there's nothing like hands-on experience, you can also learn a lot by researching hunting. Thousands of books have been written on hunting. There are also several national magazines that feature articles and stories about hunting.

Check with your state wildlife agency, too. Most wildlife agencies publish a monthly conservation magazine that features hunting articles and articles about wildlife, and many also produce books, brochures, and handouts. Wildlife agency websites are probably the best source for up-to-date information on hunting regulations.

Spending time during the rest of the year on the land where you are planning to hunt gives you a major advantage once the hunting season rolls around.

If you have a local hunter's organization or shooting club that is active in your area, you might also check if they have youth programs or youth memberships. Then get involved with their group and group projects. A hunting group can be a good place to find a mentor for hunting and to learn to shoot as well.

OUTDOOR SKILLS

Hunting means spending a lot of time outdoors. Really good hunters are deeply familiar with nature and spend as much time in it as possible. Doing this will make you a better hunter. Spend time hiking or camping during different seasons of the year to see if you're really going to enjoy being out in all kinds of weather. Not everyone does.

Choose your hiking companions wisely. It is not fun to be in the woods with someone who complains about insects, cobwebs, dirt, or snakes. Don't take foolish risks. Learn what kinds of animals to stay away from—such as rattlesnakes and bears. Avoid areas where these critters may be found until you become comfortable dealing with such situations safely.

Finally, always let other people know where you are going and when you plan to return. Give them a specific description of the area, such as the name of a hollow or a canyon. That way, if you don't return within a reasonable period of time, they will know where to look or where to send search parties. After all, it is very easy to fall, break a leg, or sprain an ankle in the woods. Common sense and good judgment should always prevail when you're in the great outdoors.

SHOOTING SKILLS

You will still need a lot of practice to become a skilled marksman. Target practice, therefore, becomes a necessary activity. Just setting out some tin cans or pinning up a paper target and blazing away is not the best way to learn. First, safety precautions must be taken. Remember to build a backstop to keep bullets or shot from traveling beyond the target. A beginner definitely needs the supervision of an experienced adult marksman.

Joining a hunting club is one way to accomplish this, since most clubs have some type of safe shooting facilities available for their members. Another way might be to join a National Rifle Association (NRA) shooting team. There you will get the valuable assistance of trained coaches.

RIFLE COMPETITIONS

The NRA and other organizations host competitions in which you can test your marksmanship skills against those of others. Rifle competitions are generally organized by what sort of firearm you will be using.

SMALL-BORE RIFLE COMPETITIONS

Competition in this category involves shooting small-bore rifles (such as the .22 caliber) at paper targets at different ranges and

These sportsmen are taking part in the NRA National Outdoor Rifle & Pistol Championships. The championships feature dozens of different events.

47

from different positions (such as lying down, sitting, and standing). Shooting may be done at indoor or outdoor ranges. These competitions are a great way for beginners to learn the basics of marksmanship.

HIGH-POWERED RIFLE COMPETITIONS

These competitions are held at outdoor ranges. Some are very formal, with strict rules governing what participants are allowed to do. Others—often those conducted by local sportsmen and sportswomen—are more causal. Whether the event is formal or casual, range safety rules are always strictly observed. High-powered rifle contestants may shoot from a bench rest at paper targets that are anywhere from 100 yards (91 m) to more than 1,000 yards (914 m) away. Some contests involve shooting at moving targets from off-hand standing positions.

MUZZLE-LOADING COMPETITIONS

These competitions involve shooting with primitive firearm types, such as flintlock rifles, that were used in past centuries. Many black powder shoots are gala events with the participants dressing in frontier or mountaineer clothing. Often shooting is done off-hand, but some matches are done only with heavy bench-rest target rifles. Novelty shooting is a hallmark of these events. One event involves shooting a soft lead ball at the edge of an axe that cuts the ball in two, causing each piece to break a balloon on either side of the

ARCHERY COMPETITIONS

Archery shooting may be done using several kinds of targets, from traditional bull's-eyes to Styrofoam models of game animals. Field archery courses involve shooting at replicas of game animals under actual field conditions. For example, contestants may walk through a wooded trail and shoot at targets set up at different ranges or even shoot from tree stands.

There are also competitions featuring 3-D archery simulations. These re-create actual hunting situations with electronic machines that project hunting scenes onto a background, like a movie.

blade. Tomahawk and knife throwing are regular features at these kinds of competitions.

SHOTGUN COMPETITIONS

The main sorts of shotgun competitions are trapshooting, skeet, and sporting clays. They all involve shooting at flying targets, which are generally known as clay pigeons. In trapshooting, shooters take up a position behind a low structure that houses a machine that launches clay pigeons into the air. When the shooter is ready, he or she yells, "Pull!" A clay disk is released and the shooter tries to break it in the air by shooting at it. Disks are released at various speeds, angles, and heights. The shooter who breaks the most clay pigeons wins.

Skeet is a little different in that a group of shooters stand in a semicircle. Two trap houses sit to the right and left of the shooters' positions. One is high and one low. Clay birds are hurled across in front of the shooters in combinations of singles, doubles, or triples. The shooters rotate through the five firing positions to alter their perspectives.

In sporting clay competitions, real hunting situations are simulated. Machines that launch clay pigeons are hidden in a vari-

The disks of clay that people shoot are known as clay pigeons. The reason they are called this is because, in the past, people used to release live pigeons for target shooting.

ety of field types, such as in a thick aspen wood or beside a pond. Each station simulates a different type of hunting scenario. Various sizes of clay disks are used to imitate different types of game. Some bounce along the ground like a cottontail would, while others sail through the thick brush or come right at the shooter the way a grouse or dove might. Still others flush straight up like a pheasant or mallard.

FINDING EVENTS

The National Rifle Association sponsors one of the best competitions for young people through a program called Youth Hunter Education Challenge. Although the competition is open to single contestants, local sportsman's clubs usually cosponsor the program. Regional, state, and national championships are conducted annually. The challenge involves outdoor rifle, shotgun, and archery shooting at simulated game animals under actual field conditions. To enter the competition, a young hunter must have completed the hunter-training program in his or her state or province.

Competitions are not the only hunting-related events. Many state and national organizations offer special incentive programs for youths interested in hunting, including the National Wild Turkey Association's Jake's Day event. Youth Field Day events are offered in several states at local sportsman's clubs. Ask fellow hunters what events they have enjoyed participating in.

RESPONSIBLE HUNTING

T he concept of "fair chase" has always played a big role in North American sport hunting. Fair chase involves following hunting laws and adhering to ethical, sportsman-like hunting methods, ones that do not give hunters too much of an advantage over the animals they are hunting. The emphasis many hunters put on fair chase shows how responsible hunters can—and should—be.

HUNTING AND THE ENVIRONMENT

Responsible hunters understand that the animals they hunt are part of the natural world. They also understand that people have done things that threaten the ecosystems in which those animals live and see the necessity of the laws that protect them.

This Missouri hunter is tagging a deer he shot. Hunting tag requirements help wildlife agencies control the number of animals that are killed each year.

These include laws that limit when, where, and what people are allowed to hunt.

If an animal is endangered, hunting it is against the law. Bag limit laws keeps the populations of animals that are not presently in danger of dying out at healthy levels by setting a limit on the number of animals of a particular species any given hunter can kill. Along with a daily bag limit, many states and provinces limit how many animals a hunter can take in a season—often by issuing a limited number of tags to hunters. You are most likely to need tags if you are hunting large game, such as deer, moose, or bear.

CRITICS OF HUNTING

There are plenty of people in the United States who do not support hunting. Some people believe that killing animals is wrong under any circumstances. Others accept the killing of animals for food, but think that to do so for sport is wrong. They argue that, even if hunters eat the meat, their main goal is their own enjoyment.

People who support hunting in general may also be opposed to certain forms of it. For example, many hunters are against baiting, or putting out food to draw animals to you. People also argue that the use of certain kinds of firearms or bows—such as automatic weapons and crossbows—violates the principles of fair chase.

A PERSONAL DECISION

Hunting means taking the life of an animal, and you have to feel comfortable with that. Talk to hunters in your family or community about how they view their role. You will probably find that they have respect for the wildlife they hunt. You may also find that hunting in your area actually helps to control problems of animal overpopulation.

After learning more, you may still decide that you do not want to become a hunter. If you do so, that is completely OK. If friends or family expect you to hunt, explain to them

If you decide that you do want to be a hunter, you're likely to find a whole community of other hunters out there who would be happy to welcome you into their midst.

why hunting in not for you. Whatever your reason, people should respect your decision. Hunting is not an activity you should have to take part in if it makes you uncomfortable.

THE FUTURE OF HUNTING

Each hunter must assume personal responsibility for his or her actions. Hunters must always ensure that certain principles, such as fair chase, are not violated. They must be committed to obeying all season and bag limits, along with all the other regulations that govern hunting. Finally, they must take an active part in helping to police their own ranks by taking a strong stand against poaching and other wildlife crime. They should never be shy about reporting those who deliberately violate the rules. Responsible hunting practices are what guarantee the future of the practice—both by demonstrating that hunters are trustworthy and conscientious and by ensuring that there will still be quarry around to hunt in the years to come.

ACTION The way in which a gun is loaded and fired.

BLIND A simple shelter used to conceal a hunter from wild game.

CALIBER A measurement of the diameter of a bullet or the inside diameter of a rifle's barrel.

CAMOUFLAGE Something that helps a person or animal blend into the natural surroundings.

CLAY PIGEON A clay disk used as a target for shotgun shooting.

CROSSBOW A bow fixed crosswise on a stock with a trigger release.

FLINTLOCK An ignition system seen in muzzle-loading firearms. It involves using a piece of flint to send a shower of sparks into a pan of priming powder to ignite the powder in the barrel of the gun.

GAME Wild animals that are hunted for food and sport.

GAUGE A measurement of the size of a shotgun or shotgun shell.

GLOBAL POSITIONING SYSTEM A handheld computer that can calculate one's exact location using a global positioning satellite.

HABITAT A place containing all the necessary requirements for a particular species to live, such as food, water, shelter, and space.

MUZZLE LOADER A firearm that requires the powder charge and projectiles to be loaded individually by pushing them down the barrel with a ramrod.

POACHING Hunting game illegally, such as hunting out of season or taking game that is listed as an endangered species.

QUARRY An animal that is being hunted.

SAFETY A blocking device that prevents the trigger from pulling or blocks the firing pin or hammer from striking a chambered shell.

SCAT Animal fecal droppings.

SPORT HUNTING Hunting for fun, rather than because one needs to get food.

TOPOGRAPHICAL MAP A kind of map that includes terrain types and elevations.

Canadian Shooting Sports Association
116 Galaxy Boulevard
Etobicoke, ON M9W 4Y6
Canada
(888) 873-4339
Website: http://cssa-cila.org
Dedicated to the promotion of shooting sports in Canada, this group is a big supporter of the rights of gun owners. It also provides regular firearm training courses and sponsors shooting events.

Ducks Unlimited, Inc.
One Waterfowl Way
Memphis, TN 38120
(800) 453-8257
Website: http://www.ducks.org
Established in 1937, this organization focuses on the conservation of waterfowl habitats. It is a great source of information about wetland ecosystems, waterfowl species, and waterfowl hunting. Along with an annual national convention, it also holds dozens of smaller events around the United States each year.

Ministry of Natural Resources and Forestry
Information Centre
300 Water Street
Peterborough ON K9J 8M5
Canada
(800) 667-1940
http://www.ontario.ca/government/about-ministry-natural-resources-and-forestry
The government agency in charge of protecting the natural resources in Canada's most populous province, this ministry employs more than three thousand people. It has passed many significant pieces of legislation on hunting and land conservation.

National Rifle Association of America
11250 Waples Mill Road
Fairfax, VA 22030
(800) 672-3888
Website: http://hservices.nra.org
Founded in the state of New York in 1871, this long-lived organization has helped develop hunter education programs and continues to be involved in hunter safety and education efforts. It also hosts a wide array of shooting competitions. The National Rife Association is an outspoken supporter for the rights of gun owners.

National Wild Turkey Federation
Post Office Box 530
Edgefield, SC 29824
(800) 843-6983
Website: http://www.nwtf.org
Many turkey hunters belong to the NWTF, an organization that has been instrumental in efforts to protect turkey habitat and help the wild turkey population return to a healthy level. The group is a good resource for learning about every aspect of turkey hunting and finding turnkey-hunting events in your area.

Pheasants Forever
1783 Buerkle Circle
St. Paul, MN 55110
(877) 773-2070
Website: https://www.pheasantsforever.org
Pheasant hunters formed this organization dedicated to the preservation of pheasant populations and habitat in 1982. Today, the group has more than seven hundred local chapters in the United States and Canada. The organization has been able to preserve more than 170,000 acres (68,800 hectares) of habitat.

U.S. Fish and Wildlife Service
1849 C Street NW
Washington, DC 20240
(800) 344-9453
Website: http://www.fws.gov
This federal agency is tasked with stewarding the fish and wildlife resources of the United States. It leads habitat conservation efforts, protects endangered species, operates an extensive system of national wildlife refuges, and has field offices throughout the country.

Whitetails Unlimited
National Headquarters
2100 Michigan Street
Sturgeon Bay, WI 54235
(800) 274-5471
Website: http://www.whitetailsunlimited.com
The goals of this national organization are to educate the public about whitetail hunting, to protect and preserve whitetail habitat, and to preserve the American whitetail-hunting tradition. The group's website is a good place to find local chapters and deer camps.

WEBSITES

Because of the changing nature of Internet links, Rosen Publishing has developed an online list of websites related to the subject of this book. This site is updated regularly. Please use this link to access the list:

http://www.rosenlinks.com/OUT/Hunt

Bestul, Scott. *Field & Stream's Guide to Hunting Whitetail.* New York, NY: Gareth Stevens Publishing, 2015.

Cassell, Jay. *The Ultimate Guide to Bowhunting Skills, Tactics, and Techniques.* New York, NY: Skyhorse Publishing, 2011.

Eye, Ray. *Ray Eye's Turkey Hunting Bible: The Tips, Tactics, and Secrets of a Professional Turkey Hunter.* New York, NY: Skyhorse Publishing, 2012.

Johnson, Chuck. *Training the Versatile Hunting Dog.* Belgrade, MT: Wilderness Adventures Press, Inc., 2013.

MacWelch, Tim. T*he Hunting & Gathering Survival Manual: 221 Primitive & Wilderness Survival Skills.* San Francisco, CA: Weldon Owen, 2013.

McIntosh, Michael. *Shotguns & Shooting.* Lanham, MD: Derrydale Press, 2014.

Meyer, Susan. *Hunting Dogs: Different Breeds and Special Purposes.* New York, NY: Rosen Central, 2012.

Nguyen, Jenny, and Rick Wheatley. *Hunting for Food: Guide to Harvesting, Field Dressing, and Cooking Wild Game.* Iola, WI: Living Ready, 2015.

Nickens, T. Edward. *The Total Outdoorsman Manual.* 10th Anniversary Edition. San Francisco, CA: Weldon Owen, 2013.

Sparano, Vincent T. *Tales of Woods and Waters: An Anthology of Classic Hunting and Fishing Stories.* New York, NY: Skyhorse Publishing, 2015.

Steier, David. *Guns 101: A Beginner's Guide to Buying and Owning Firearms.* New York, NY: Skyhorse Publishing, 2011.

ABOUT THE AUTHORS

Joe Gaspar is a lover of the great outdoors and has spent many hours in the woods and fields of the New England and Mid-Atlantic regions. He is a strong proponent of responsible hunting practices and habitat conservation.

Jack Weaver is a graduate of the Pennsylvania Game Commission's Ross Leffler School of Conservation. He served as a wildlife conservation officer for the Pennsylvania Game Commission (PGC) between 1969 and 1999. He has written extensively for the PGC's official magazine, *Pennsylvania Game News*, and is also the author of *Phantoms of the Woods*. Throughout his career, Weaver worked extensively with Pennsylvania's Hunter Education.

PHOTO CREDITS

Cover, p. 1 Steve Oehlenschlager/Shutterstock.com; pp. 4-5 ands456/ iStock/Thinkstock; p. 7 Private Collection/Peter Newark American Pictures/ Bridgeman Images; p. 10 Photo 12/Universal Images Group/Getty Images; p. 12 Jean-Erick Pasquier/Gamma-Rapho/Getty Images; p. 15 Fuse/Thinkstock; p. 18 BulentGrp/iStock/Thinkstock; p. 20 Mike Cherim/iStock/Thinkstock; p. 23 Bruce MacQueen/Shutterstock.com; p. 27 MyLoupe/Universal Images Group/Getty Images; p. 28 Styles Bridges/Shutterstock.com; p. 30 Jason Lugo/ E+/Getty Images; p. 33 Bruce Gifford/Moment Mobile/Getty Images; pp. 36, 53 © AP Images; pp. 38, 42 RubberBall Productions/Brand X Pictures/Getty Images; p. 44 Stockbyte/Thinkstock; p. 47 Bob Rosato/Sports Illustrated/ Getty Images; p. 50 Kevin Steele/Aurora/Getty Images; p. 55 © James Smedley/Alamy; cover and interior pages Iwona Grodzka/iStock/Thinkstock (twig frame), AKIRA/amanaimagesRF/Thinkstock (wood frame)

Photo researcher: Karen Huang